Dancing Hands
Signs of Learning™

Story by
Mary Belle Harwich & John Hay

Pictures by
Robert Wapahi

Title by Murray David Harwich III

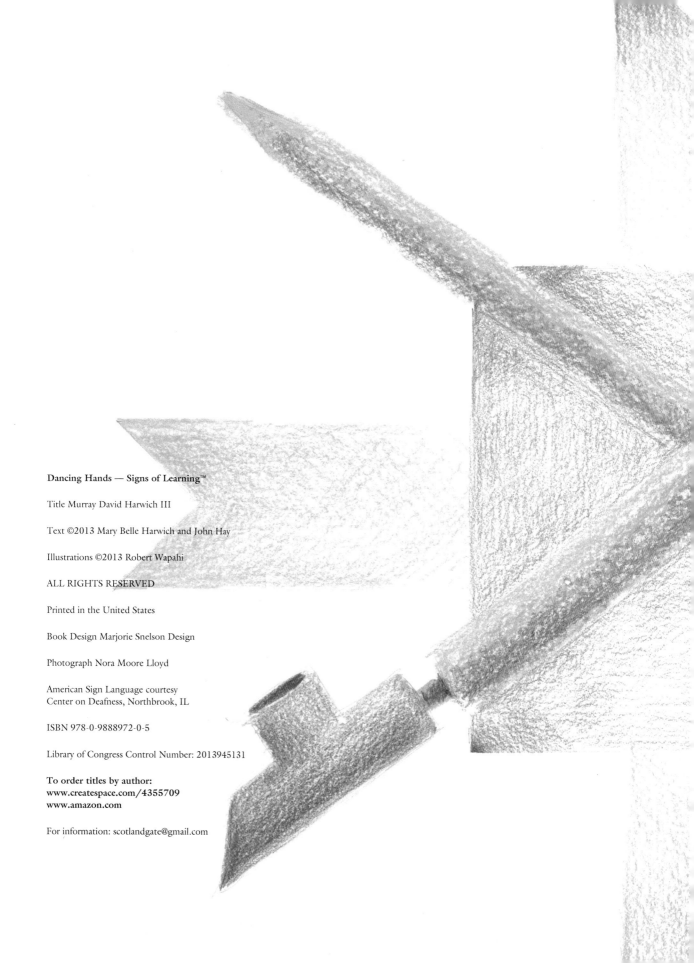

Dancing Hands — Signs of Learning™

Title Murray David Harwich III

Text ©2013 Mary Belle Harwich and John Hay

Illustrations ©2013 Robert Wapahi

Printed in the United States

Book Design Marjorie Snelson Design

Photograph Nora Moore Lloyd

American Sign Language courtesy
Center on Deafness, Northbrook, IL

ISBN 978-0-9888972-0-5

Library of Congress Control Number: 2013945131

To order titles by author:
www.createspace.com/4355709
www.amazon.com

For information: scotlandgate@gmail.com

Hundreds of years ago, when the pioneers came to America, the First People of the land taught them a sign language. In this way they were able to understand each other. Then silently the First People showed the settlers the ways of the trees, the forest, the animals, food, shelter, clothing, and all of the things that were… and so helped them begin their life in a new world.

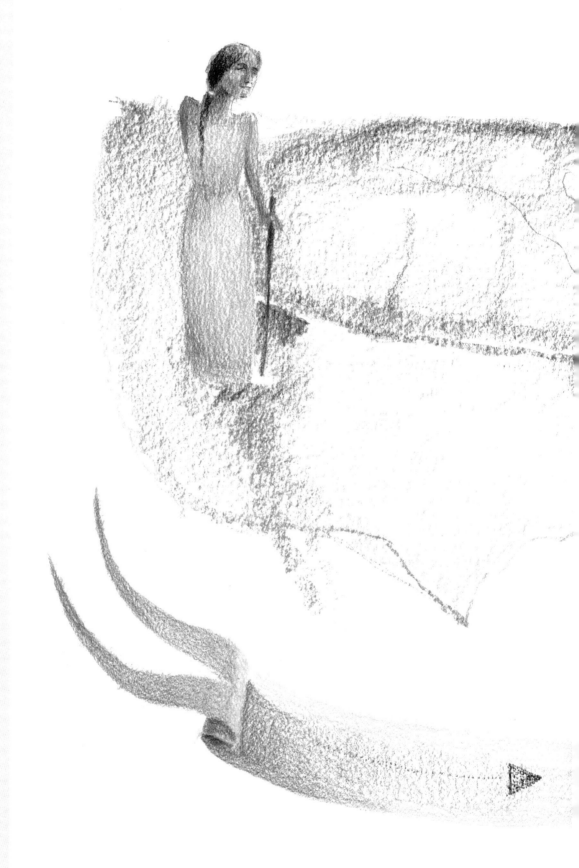

America,
vast and
beautiful —

2

A
is for
America

Bear and
Buffalo
roam the
land.

B
is for
Buffalo

Swift
Canoes
cut the
fresh
water.

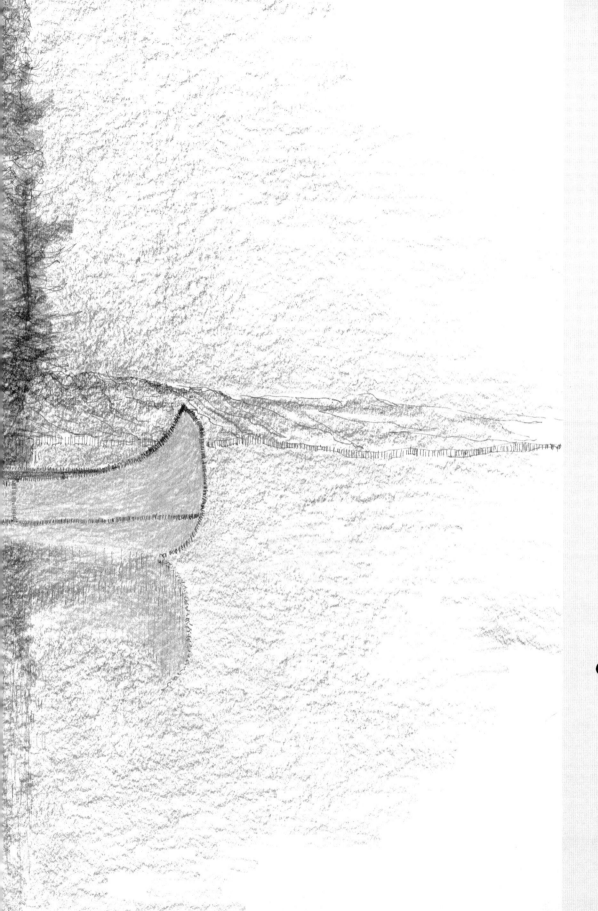

C
is for
Canoe

And Deer
run the
edges
of the cane
brake.

8

D
is for
Deer

The Eagle
high above
watches
with a
clear eye.

E

is for

Eagle

Under the
trees,
tremendous
and full,
sunlight
dapples the
Forest.

F
is for
Forest

The Guide,
  leading,
finds a path
to the river.

14

G

is for
Guide

Silently,
the Hunter
follows
tracks in
the soft
earth.

16

H
is for
Hunter

17

Ice closes
over the
waters.
Winter
has come.

I
is for
Ice

In January,
under the
bright
Wolf
Moon,
animals
hunt
for food.

J
is for
January

21

Through
the
woodlands
of
Kentucky,
the
pioneers
come,
looking
for a place
to make
their home.

22

K
is for
Kentucky

With a
swing
of an axe,
a tree falls:
soon
there is
a cabin
on the
Land.

24

L
is for
Land

The
Moonlight,
shining
silver,
lights up
the forest
trail.

26

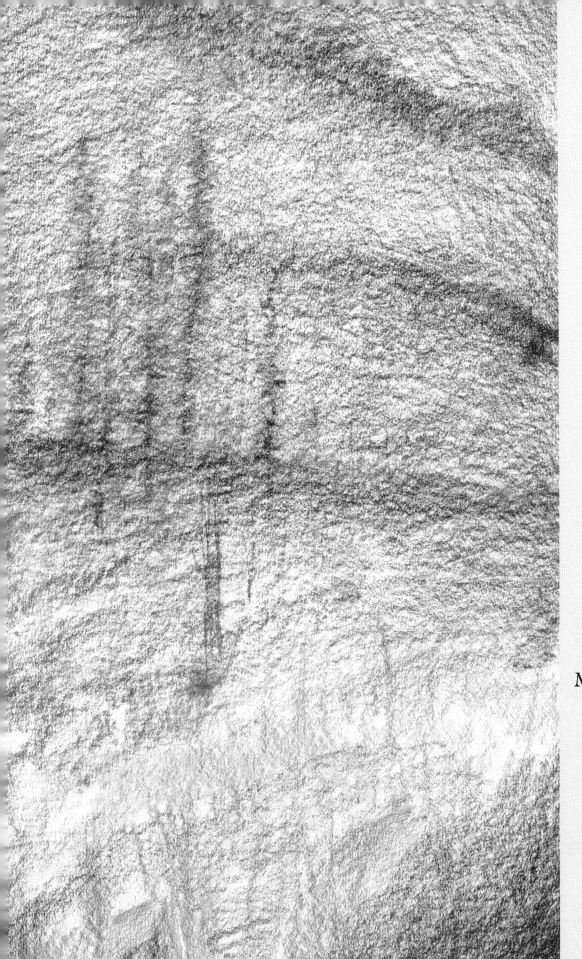

M
is for
Moonlight

A
New
World,
a place
to make
a brave
beginning.

N
is for
New World

The Ohio,
a great
river of
open and
moving
waters,
greets
them.

O

is for

Ohio

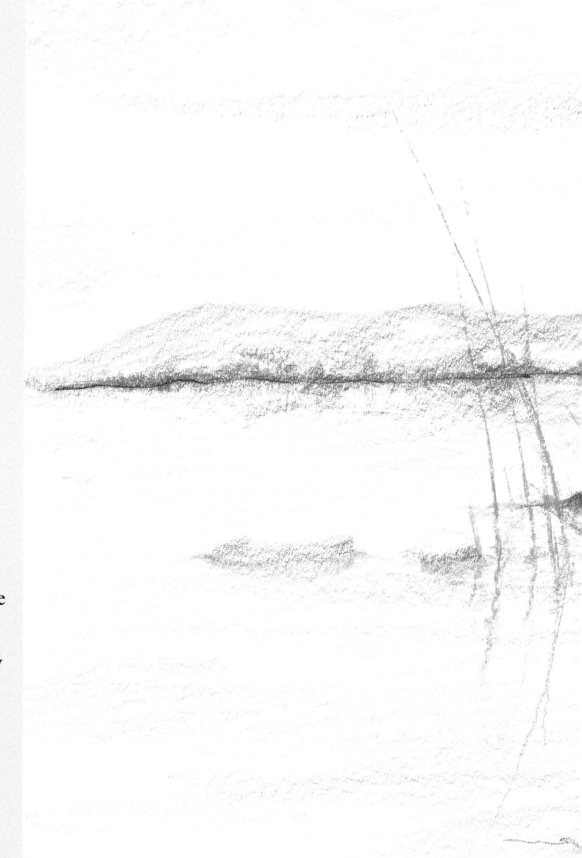

The
Porcupine
brings
his family
down to
the river
to drink.

32

P
is for
Porcupine

Quest, a search for meadows and streams of running water.

Q
is for
Quest

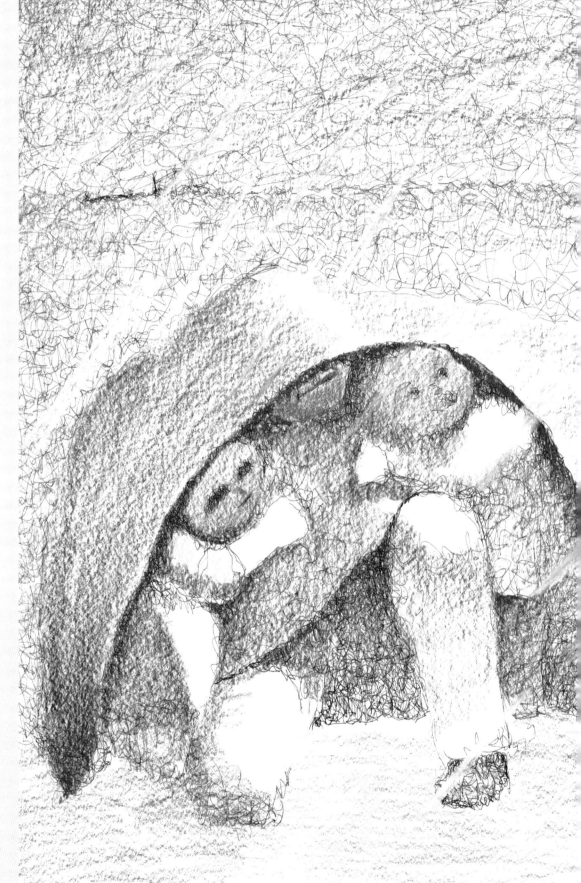

Rain
and sun
touch the
earth —
new life
follows.

36

R

is for

Rain

Settlers
find
places
to live
in the
wilderness.

S

is for
Settlers

Great
chiefs
taught the
people to
be strong.

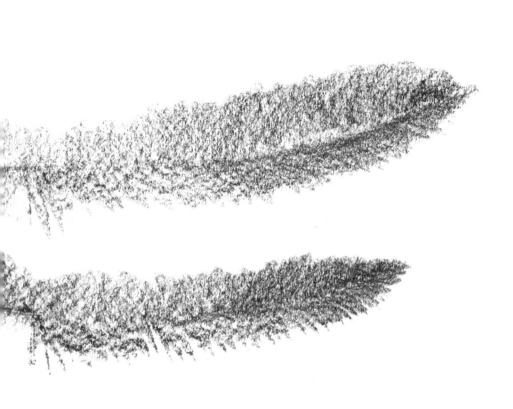

T
is for
Teacher

The
best of
everyone
wishes to
Understand
each
other's
way.

42

U
is for
Understand

From the
Native
Villages,
from the
log cabins
of the
settlers,
great cities
begin
to grow.

44

V
is for
Villages

And the
ways
of the
Wilderness
are passing.

46

W
is for
Wilderness

47

X, a sign,
to mark
hidden
trails to
follow.

X

is for a
mark

The Year
goes by:
winter,
spring,
summer,
fall — a
time to
journey —
a time to
learn many
things.

50

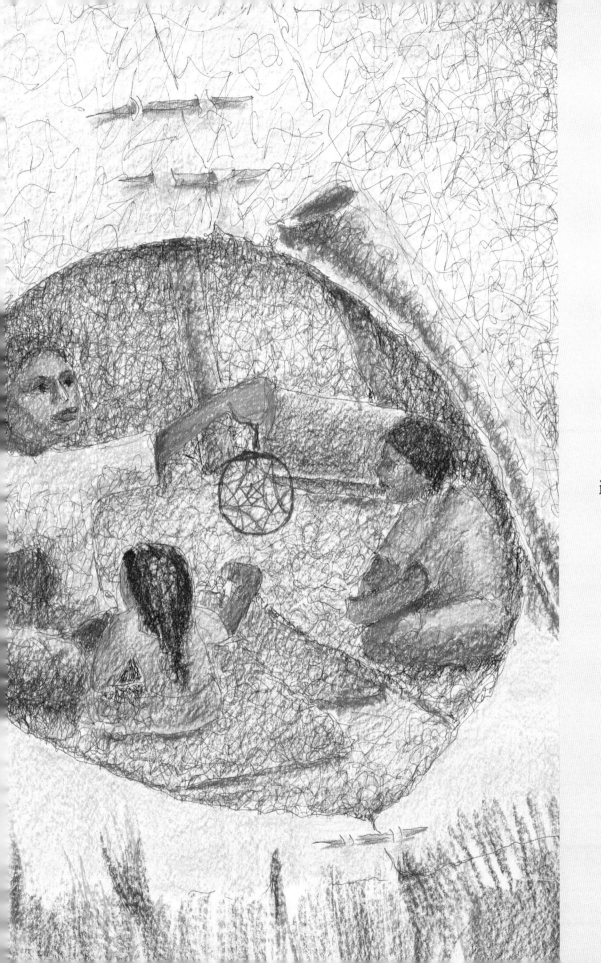

Y

is for

Year

The
thunder
rumbles
and
lightning
Zigzags
across the
sky — all
look up.

Z
is for
Zigzag

To make a sign is an ancient way of reaching out to another person. In signing, you may use your hands and fingers, even the expression on your face. You can speak without making a sound, using your whole body. You can say what is in your mind and heart. It is a journey into another world of understanding.

America

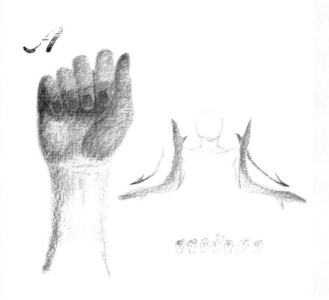

Ikce wi costa (Our land)

Buffalo

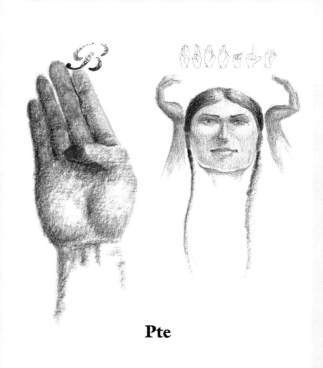

Pte

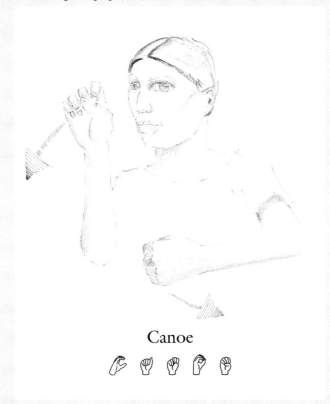

Canoe

Chon **ha** wa da

Deer

Ta ca

Eagle

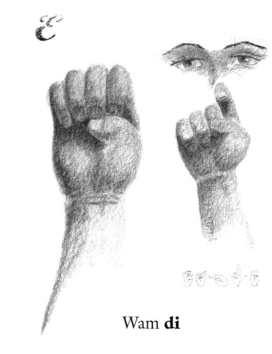

Wam **di**

Forest

Chon **ton** ka (Exploding and
popping thing made of wood)

Guide

Usok **chon** ye

Hunter

We ne za

Ice

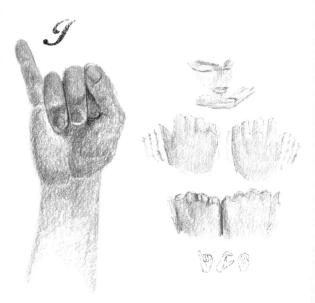

Ca gah

January

We **te** he (The time of trees popping)

Kentucky

To pezi (Blue Grass)

Land

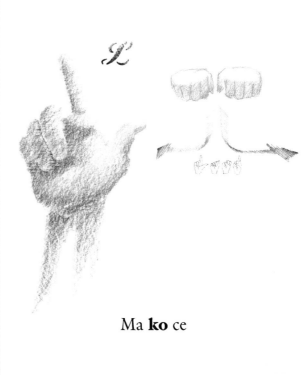

Ma **ko** ce

61

Moonlight

Hon **we**

New World

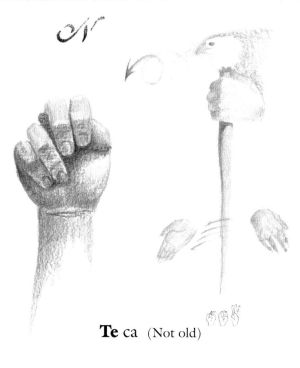

Te ca (Not old)

Ohio

Mni (Moving waters)

Porcupine

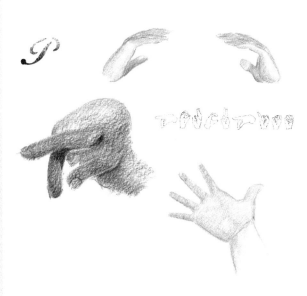

Pa **hin**

Quest

A **ke** ta

Rain

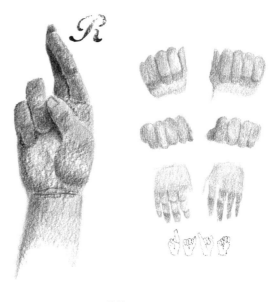

Ma **ga** zu

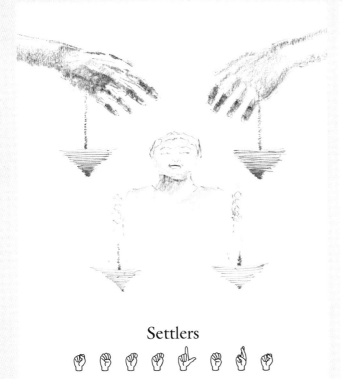

Settlers

Wa si **cu** (People not like us)

Teacher

Wa **oons** pe keya
(One who shares our ways of life)

Understand

Oh **ka** ne ga   (Are you following my words)

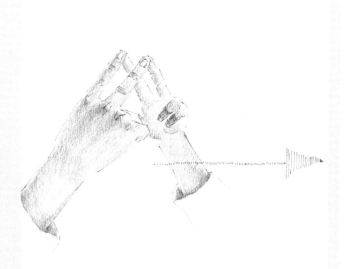

Villages

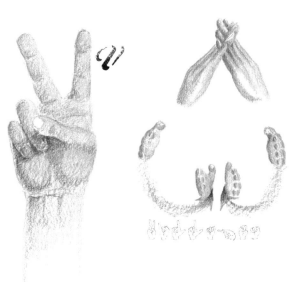

We **cho** te

Wilderness

Wa **to** da

X, a mark

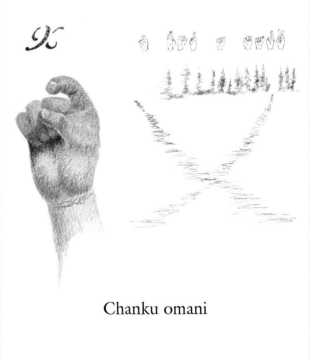

Chanku omani

Year

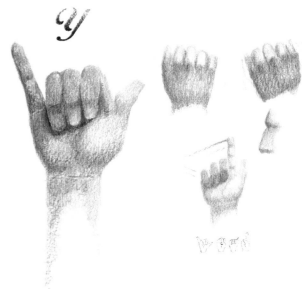

O ma ka (First snow, end of year, beginning of story time till spring)

Zigzag

Yuk **don** kdon key a
(Mark that lightning makes)

Circling winds

carry forever

an act of kindness...

Robert Wapahi, Dakota, was born in 1945 on the
Santee Indian Reservation in South Dakota. Pen and ink
has become his favorite medium with oils coming in at a
close second. Of note, most compositions are horizontal
or landscape, which is only fitting for someone from the
Great Plains. Robert is also an accomplished musician
and traditional storyteller. His work is represented in private
collections and he has participated in group exhibitions
and solo shows.

Made in the USA
Charleston, SC
22 July 2015